FEAST OF THE ANIMALS

AN ALASKA BESTIARY

Volume II

FEAST OF THE ANIMALS

AN ALASKA BESTIARY
Volume II

By SHEILA NICKERSON

WOOD ENGRAVINGS by DALE DeARMOND

OLD HARBOR PRESS
SITKA · ALASKA

International Standard Book Number: 0-9615529-8-0
Library of Congress Catalog Number: 86-62524
OLD HARBOR PRESS, Publishers and Printers
P.O. BOX 97, SITKA, ALASKA 99835

For Raven --
  who made it all.

CONTENTS

viii

INTRODUCTION

The title of this book comes from the Eskimo observance of a feast day to honor the animals and birds who have let themselves be killed so that people can have food and clothing and the many artifacts they make from the hides and bones and beaks. At one point in the ceremonies the hunters return to the sea the bladders of the animals they have killed so that the *innuas* (souls) can return to them and there will be more animals the following year.

Dale DeArmond

Sometimes I visit

in the neighborhood of man.

Sometimes there is something there

that pulls me, scents that bloom

bigger than berries, a promise.

There, in the alleys, streets,

and on the porches where they live,

they chase me, as if I had grown

giant as the darkness of the woods

with teeth as sharp as winter cold.

Black Bear

I am the blossom of the richness

of the woods, the flesh of good season.

I bring forth my child spotted

like the floor of the summer forest,

and the forest is my winter roof.

The words I whisper (you never hear me speak)

are blueberry, spruce, hemlock, moss.

Silence is winterkill,

the untracked snow.

Sitka Black-tailed Deer

5

All winter, we listen to our trees,

never straying.

But in April, we change.

Rising up, we plummet, strut, drum,

dancing with the wild sap—

a courtship all must envy.

With summer, it is done.

We are content

to fold ourselves in spruce

and wait upon our trees.

Spruce Grouse

Kelp. You gave me kelp

and the sweet meat of shells.

Mother, I take my child in my arms

and hold her in a lullaby of fur,

a feast of sea urchin,

the roll of the rocky shore.

Kelp. You gave me kelp,

and I give my child love.

Sea Otter

9

I am the dark head

in the forest creek

looking for fish or mouse.

So fast I am, that even after death,

if you have my skin and skull

and set me free, I will hunt

whatever you want,

however deep its hole.

Mink

11

I keep to the open,

hunt by light.

Waiting on hummocks,

I appear no more

than a patch of snow.

In the season of lemmings

I grow fat.

When lemmings leave

and the sun flies away,

I go, too,

flying to delicious fields,

wherever they lead.

Snowy Owl

I can kill a crab with venom,

feast on its flesh.

With no bones, I am free.

I can change shape, color,

give up an arm, shoot ink,

flow into a small hole.

But when I hatch my young, I die.

There is no escape from the egg cave.

Octopus

We are the maskmakers.

We pick and choose

from feathers and fur.

Hiding, we imitate, call down.

But always in the dancing dark

we know that something moves

beyond the shadowed walls--

something like our mother,

something without mask

that calls us from the dance.

Maskmaker

I live in rocks, collecting grass.

Once, when all the animals disappeared from the world,

I took the starving people to their hiding place.

I sang before that mountain.

The animals came out. The sun came out.

The people were no longer hungry.

Now, I farm hay from tundra flowers.

My rocky barns are always full,

never host to hunger.

Collared Pica

I am always masked,

ready for the dance.

Watch me dive from cliffs,

fly under water.

Watch me, watch me,

on the sea's great stage.

And afterwards,

in the final act,

my beak becomes a rattle

for a dancer's glove.

Puffin

In our paws, communion with snow.

We know where danger is—

soft spots on the ice,

bad places in the night.

Our joy is in the village beyond.

We do not let our driver

be misguided by spirits

tempting him away from home.

Malamute

I am hunger on legs,

threading the loom of life.

Eater and eaten,

I burn through the dark of the earth.

Seizer and seized, I survive--

talons, teeth, and deep cold--

keeping the world on its course,

keeping the stars in the sky.

Shrew

Bonaparte's, Glaucous, Black-backed,

Iceland, Ivory, Ross's,

Sabine's, Herring, and Slaty-backed:

I come in many shapes but am the same.

They call me scavenger,

but, Mother, you gave me all the coast

to guard, to clean, the tides to chase,

a work endless as the waves.

Sea Gull

I go by many names,

from King to Dog.

Really I am waterspout or rainbow,

collector of colors,

throwing my silver self

out of the sea for joy.

Everywhere, they chase me

but do not know my ways.

Salmon

They have made of me a monster,

Kooshdaka, taking the souls of men.

But when we leap, four of us together,

onto the evening dock, playing games till dark,

the child of man watches and wants to join.

Land Otter

I feast on birch, aspen, willow—

if not too high.

After the winter snows—

if not too deep—

I find my way to water,

seeking sweet hidden greens.

Mother, I am large as trees,

but you left the wolf circling me,

and the bear—hungry, always hungry.

Moose

In April, I return from the south

on the wings of the sandhill crane.

This fact has been disputed,

but how else would I manage

the miles of mountain and sea,

keeping to a schedule

as certain as daffodils?

Hummingbird

35

I own two sets of clothes,

wear myth on my back,

know the track of every vole:

the tunnel heart of earth.

When man wants extra strength,

he hangs my skin around his neck.

Weasel

Like fire out of the northern woods

I shoot, following the ways of mice.

The map of the world is all in my nose.

I cannot lose my way.

Red Fox

They call me gypsy fruiteater,

but I know each stand of mountain ash

and how to reach them just before a storm,

their berries bright as my wingtips.

And when I've had my fill,

I lift with my kind

in an arc of winter bells,

calling the cold to follow

where I lead.

Bohemian Waxwing

I know the deepest holes.

My mother told me

I would never lack darkness

in which to hide and grow

the whitest flesh

in all the northern seas.

Out of my black heaven

comes the power to move tides

and call small fishes home.

All I have to do is wait

patiently on ocean peaks

and in the mouths of autumn creeks.

Halibut

Because I am among the smallest,

I have been given extra strength.

I taste the heart of summer,

hold the seasons in my paws.

My eyes see shadows on the moon.

I hear the crackle of a fern.

My nose recreates the history of the world.

The track I leave, with claw and tail,

is more beautiful than frost in winter grass.

Mouse

Brothers and sisters of the snow,

we grow white in our round, slow way,

feeding in shallows when we can.

If we move slower than the ice and cannot breathe,

we drown. But when we're free, we sing,

whistling our way across the northern sea.

Mother, you gave us rivers

to explore. We travel the Yukon

past its salt, even to Alaska's heart.

Beluga

Flying under the sign

of the Northern Cross

I hold in my throat

the notes of a thousand legends.

Wherever you live, you have heard them:

prophecy, spell, transformation.

But silence is best--

stretching into the watery stems

for the tenderness I seek:

the song of wild celery,

of eelgrass, lily, and sedge.

Tundra Swan

49

Bold as truth,

I circle the frozen night,

cutting out the weak of the herds.

I have chosen one mate,

I have remembered the old of the pack.

I do not live in the fairy tales

read by the children of man

but in my own community,

a moving round of care.

Wolf

My blood runs blue with iodine.

My ten legs hug the ocean floor.

Nobody knows where I go or why.

Mother, you gave me the power

to travel undetected.

I keep the secret hidden,

like my unexpected heart.

Only the shaman knows

my deep, sharp ways.

Crab

53

The secret that you taught me, Mother,

is to go UP, always UP.

Even the youngest lamb knows this.

But the wolf does, too,

always working to force us DOWN

into the valley of his teeth.

Dall Sheep

COLOPHON

This book was hand set in 14-point Bembo type printed on an Original Heidelberg platen press and Mohawk Letterpress Text paper. Two thousand five hundred copies are bound in Fox River Circa '83 paper.

A hard cover, limited edition signed by the author and the artist, is bound in Canson Mi Tientes paper, with Ingres Antique end sheets. Each includes a print hand pulled by the artist from the original wood engraving. They are hand sewn in the Japanese style and materials used are archival quality. It is limited to 50 copies.